Men-at-Arms • 155

The Knights of Christ

Terence Wise • Illustrated by Richard Scollins

Series editor Martin Windrow

First published in Great Britain in 1984 by
Osprey Publishing, Midland House, West Way, Botley,
Oxford OX2 0PH, UK
443 Park Avenue South, New York, NY 10016, USA
Email: info@ospreypublishing.com

British Library Cataloguing in Publication Data

Wise, Terence
    The Knights of Christ.—(Men-at-Arms-series; 155)
    1. Knights and knighthood—Europe—History
    I. Title   II. Series
    305.5'2   CR4509

    ISBN-13: 978-0-85045-604-2

Series Editor: MARTIN WINDROW

Filmset in Great Britain
Printed in China through World Print Ltd.

07 08 09 10 11   30 29 28 27 26 25 24 23 22 21

FOR A CATALOGUE OF ALL BOOKS PUBLISHED BY
OSPREY MILITARY AND AVIATION PLEASE CONTACT:

NORTH AMERICA
Osprey Direct, C/o Random House Distribution Center,
400 Hahn Road, Westminster, MD 21157, USA
E-mail: info@ospreydirect.com

ALL OTHER REGIONS
Osprey Direct UK, P.O. Box 140,
Wellingborough, Northants, NN8 2FA, UK
E-mail: info@ospreydirect.co.uk

www.ospreypublishing.com

The Knights of Christ

The Church Militant

The primitive Christian Church condemned war on principle, regarding it as an evil sin no matter at what level or for what purpose it was waged. When Constantine I established toleration of Christianity throughout the Roman Empire in AD 313, this immediately created a schism, for the very survival of the empire was dependent upon war. The Eastern Empire accepted war as justified in defence of the faith, and its adoption of militaristic saints such as St George illustrates this. On the other hand, the Roman Church in the West remained firm in its belief that all war was evil, although by the time of Augustine (354–430) it had become accepted that one side might have 'just cause' for war, and individual soldiers taking part in such wars were absolved.

By the time of Pope Gregory the Great (P. 590–604), the West had adopted the interesting idea that heretics and infidels could legitimately be converted to Christianity by force; but it was not until the Carolingian wars against the Saxons in the second half of the 8th century that Christian leaders were able to convert a political war into a religious one under this guise. Meanwhile, the Church had been growing wealthy, and the Saracen invasions of Spain and France in the early 8th century had posed a threat to that wealth—indeed, to Christianity itself. Now the Roman Church could also support war in defence of the faith; and henceforth war and Church went hand in hand, with Mass said before battle, and the relics of saints carried before the troops to inspire them in 'God's work'.

This *volte-face* was in some degree due to the ancient warrior code of behaviour which had persisted in Christian Europe. Under this code a man's greatest virtues were physical strength, skill at arms, bravery, daring, loyalty to the chieftain, and solidarity within the tribe. The ideals of the

Seal of the Poor Knights of Christ.

primitive Christian Church had been diametrically opposed to such ideals. However, by channelling the martial spirit into the service of God, the brutal warrior of the past was transformed into a guardian of society. War was acceptable if it was socially useful, and the warrior codes were harnessed to create a new chivalrous spirit whereby the élite warrior class, now the nobility or ruling class, was the defender of the faith, protector of the poor and weak. This new *Miles Christianus* was to become a romantic hero to rival the heroes of the old pagan sagas: a member of an international brotherhood of a single class, with a common code of behaviour, and sharing a common code of ideals.

By the mid-11th century Pope Leo IX (P. 1049–54) was invoking war against the invading Normans in southern Italy as a means of 'liberating Christendom'. Papal blessings and banners were issued for the expedition against the Moslems in Spain in 1063, and for the invasion of 'heretic' England in 1066. All these campaigns were called

Another version of the two founders of the Templars, astride one horse, this time from Matthew Paris' *Chronica Majora*, c.1235–59. It shows the black-over-white of the Templars' banner adapted for use on knights' shields.

'holy wars', but were really political in nature; and by the time Pope Gregory VII (P. 1073–85) raised armies of papal troops by offering both financial and spiritual rewards, the pope had come to be regarded as a summoner of armies and a leader in war. Thus when Urban II called for a holy war or crusade to help the Eastern Church and the Christians in Jerusalem, the response was overwhelming. To fight for the faith had become part of the chivalric code of the warrior, and every self-respecting knight felt obliged to go on crusade—if not now, then at some time in his life. Thus the two great ideologies of medieval Europe—chivalry and Church—came together as one in the Holy Land. And here was born from that strange union perhaps the most profound expression of the dominant spirit of the Middle Ages: the 'warrior-monks' of the military orders—terms which in the not so distant past would have been contradictory.

Military Orders in the Holy Land

After Jerusalem fell to the crusaders in 1099, most of the crusaders who did not return to Europe became committed to setting up independent Christian states; and there arose the problem of how to protect the pilgrim routes to the newly won holy places, and to continue the fight against the Moslems surrounding the narrow strip of reconquered land. At this time there were only some 500 knights available to defend the kingdom of Jerusalem; obviously, they would be fatally weakened if they were thinly scattered throughout the Holy Land. Therefore, in the beginning, small bands of crusader knights voluntarily took on this task of guarding the lines of communication.

The Knights of the Temple
One such band was formed in 1115 by Hugue de Payens of Burgundy and Godfrey de Saint

Adhemar, a Fleming, who recruited seven other knights from northern France. This small voluntary association escorted pilgrims on their way from Jerusalem to Jericho, and thence to the traditional site of Jesus's baptism in the Jordan.

In 1118 this small group swore an oath before the Patriarch of Jerusalem to protect the pilgrims and observe the monastic vows of poverty, obedience and chastity. The two founder-members had originally had only one horse between them: under their vows they were to wear only those clothes which were given to them, and to own only their weapons. From these humble ideals stemmed their first name—the Poor Knights of Christ.

The Poor Knights were to some extent subsidised by the Patriarch; and when King Baldwin, impressed by their devotion, gave them quarters in a wing of the royal palace, they became in effect an unofficial police force. Their new quarters were on the supposed site of the Temple of Solomon, and this soon gave rise to another name—the Knights of the Temple, or Knights Templar.

By now the number of knights had grown, and it was felt they should be organised permanently and officially along monastic lines in accordance with their vows, but with special rules to allow for their military rôle. In about 1124 Hugue de Payens went to Europe to ask for guidance in the formulation of such rules. He was referred to the Council of the Catholic Church then sitting at Troyes in France, and it was this council which officially gave the Templars the statutes which established them as a military-religious organisation—the first official warrior-monks. Hugue had also met the greatest spiritual authority of the day—Bernard, abbot of the Cistercian monastery of Clairvaux—and the Order's statutes and rules were mostly the work of Bernard.

From the beginning, Bernard was a firm supporter of the aims of the Poor Knights and thus of the concept of warrior-monks. He recognised no contradiction between their monastic vows and their vow to kill Moslems. To him they were the first true soldiers of Christ, dedicating themselves to a duty which should be that of all Christian knights. He wrote a small pamphlet, *On the Praise of the New Knighthood*, in which he fully justified killing and violence by the knights on behalf of the faith:

'. . . the soldiers of Christ wage the battles of

Knights Templar, from a wall painting in their church at Cressac, c.1170–80. Note red cross of their Order on the breast of their long white surcoats.

their Lord in safety. They fear not the sin of killing an enemy or the peril of their own death, inasmuch as death either inflicted or borne for Christ has no taint of crime and rather merits the greater glory . . .

'First of all, there is discipline and unqualified obedience. Everybody comes and goes according to the will of the commander. Everybody wears the dresses given to him, and no one goes in search for food or garments according to his whims. They live in a community, soberly and in joy, without wife or children. And to reach evangelical perfection, they live in the same house, in the same manner, without calling anything their own, solicitous to preserve the unity of spirit in the bonds of peace.

'Impudent words, senseless occupations, immoderate laughter, whispering or even suppressed giggling are unknown. They have a

The arrest of Templars in France in 1307, from a contemporary manuscript. The cross of the Order is clearly visible on the monastic habits.

horror of chess and dice; they hate hunting; they don't even enjoy the flight of the falcon. They despise mimes, jugglers, story-tellers, dirty songs, performances of buffoons—all these they regard as vanities and inane follies. They cut their hair short because they know it is shameful for a man to wear it long. Never overdressed, they bathe rarely and are dirty and hirsute, tanned by the coat of mail and the sun.'

The rules for this first Military Order were based on those of the Cistercians. The Order's hierarchy consisted of the Grand Master, Seneschal, Deputy Master, Marshal, and the commanders or Masters of the provinces. (Jerusalem city and the kingdom of Jerusalem were separate provinces.) Each province was divided into houses known as preceptories, each with its own commander, with a knight-commander as his lieutenant. These divisions were used for command in the field as well as for the administration of monastic life.

Murder, treason, desertion, heresy, purchasing entry into the Order, plotting amongst the brothers, and revelation of the Order's secrets were all punishable by expulsion from the Order. Lesser offences such as disobedience, consorting with women, and attempting to escape from the Order were punished by loss of privileges such as having to live with the slaves, or being deprived of arms, habit and horse. Serious cases of such lesser crimes could be punished by temporary or permanent incarceration in one of the Order's castles.

On the purely military side, the rules included vows to fight to the death for the holy places of Christendom; to refuse to be ransomed if defeated; to accept every combat, no matter what the odds; to refuse quarter or ransom to the infidel; and to defend any Christian molested by infidels. These vows led to the Templars being feared beyond all other Franks by the Moslems, who retaliated by executing out of hand all Templars taken in battle.

Each knight was allowed to possess three horses and to have a squire with a fourth horse, but his armour, clothing and bedding belonged to the Order. The squires led the spare horses to the battlefield but retired once battle commenced. The knights were formed in ranks by squadrons, and there were severe penalties for any knight who broke ranks without permission.

The seal of approval from both the Pope and Bernard of Clairvaux resulted in a flood of donations for the Order, and by the time Hugue de Payens returned to Palestine in 1130 (with some 300 knights recruited for a crusade) he had been able to establish preceptories not only in Jerusalem, but in Antioch, Tripoli, Aragon and Portugal. Subsequently, preceptories were established in England, Aquitaine, Poitou, Provence, Apulia, Hungary, Germany, Sicily and Greece.

The preceptories were used to recruit and train new members, as well as to administer the properties of the Order within the province: at the peak of its power the Order owned over 9,000 feudal lordships or manors throughout Europe, and their military contingents therefore frequently included a proportion of knights and levies who owed military service to the Order in return for the lands held—fighting men who were not themselves members of the Order. Military contingents were also swollen by the admission of subordinate members to serve as sergeants; and by the admission of 'confrère knights' who served for only a short term (although sometimes for several years at a time), and who were permitted to marry, promising half their property to the Order in the event of their death. By the time of the Second Crusade the Order could muster nearly 600 knights and, together with the Knights of St John, was providing about half the total number of knights available in the Holy Land.

Their first offensive military action had been with Baldwin's expedition to Antioch to suppress rebellion within the kingdom, but from 1147 onwards they were in the forefront of the war against Islam.

By the second half of the 12th century the Order was one of the leading landowners in Syria and Palestine. Money and men continued to arrive from Europe, and in order to control and administer this vast wealth the Templars became experts in banking. By as early as 1148 they were money-lenders, despite the official Church ban on usury, and they soon had one of the largest and most efficient banking networks in the Western world. Pilgrims could now not only rely on the protection of the Templars, but could deposit funds at their local preceptory and withdraw money as required by producing letters of credit at any other Templar preceptory. Before long the Order had its own ships, and had begun to transport pilgrims to the Holy Land.

The Order's reputation and strength in the military rôle was also growing apace. In November 1177, 80 Templars with 300 other knights smashed through Saladin's army in a single crashing cavalry charge led by the Grand Master. The Moslems were completely routed, though the Grand Master was captured, refused ransom and died in prison.

His successor, Gerard de Ridefort, became notorious for his military foolhardiness and political intrigues, yet the first fault could conceivably be excused in that he merely obeyed his vows. In 1187, with only 90 Templars and 40 other knights, he charged into a Moslem force of some 7,000 cavalry. Only he and two other Templars managed to cut their way through and escape. Not long afterwards, at the battle of Hattin, he split the Christian army and led the cavalry to total defeat.

Despite these foolhardy acts the Templars, together with the Hospitaller knights, were the finest fighting force in the Holy Land; in battle they were always accorded the position of honour on the right wing, with the Hospitallers on the left.

Throughout the 13th century the Order's wealth continued to grow, but its military strength in the Holy Land began to decline—partly because fewer recruits could be found who were willing to die for the faith, and partly because of growing rivalry between the various military orders which had now

Loarre, near Huesca in Aragon, dating from the late 11th century with later additions. This was one of the Templars' main centres in Spain.

been created, dissipating their energies and even leading to Order fighting Order.

In 1243 Jerusalem was lost. The next year the Christians were decisively defeated at Gaza, and of over 300 Templars present only 36 survived. In 1250 nearly 200 Templars died in the streets of Mansurah. On this occasion the Grand Master had warned of an ambush but had been overruled by Robert of Artois: the Order had been honour-bound to follow the crusaders to their deaths.

In 1256 the Templars and Hospitallers took opposing sides in the fighting between Genoese and Venetians in Acre, and killed each other in the streets at a time when every knight was desperately needed to counter a new threat—the brilliant Turkish general Baibars. Baibars took Caesarea and Arsuf in 1265, and Antioch in 1268. A ten-year truce followed; but his successor took Tripoli in 1289, despite a gallant defence by Templars and Hospitallers. Only Acre remained in Christian hands, and here the last gallant but futile battle was fought against the overwhelming might of the united Islamic forces. After six weeks of battering by siege engines a breach was made in the outer wall. The breach was stormed by mamluks, and despite a magnificent resistance the knights were eventually compelled to withdraw to the inner line of walls. The final assault came three days later.

The Grand Master of the Templars died fighting amongst the roar of burning and collapsing buildings, but the survivors of the Order managed to withdraw into their castle at the southern end of the city and here made a last stand under their Marshal. Terms were offered, but talks broke down when a group of Moslems who had been allowed into the Temple began to assault civilians sheltering there, and the Templars—in obedience to their vows—cut the Moslems down. A second offer failed when the Marshal, who left the Temple to negotiate, was treacherously seized and beheaded. There remained only one way out, and every knight still capable of standing prepared himself for it.

The Moslems attacked the castle with fire-bombs, catapults and mines. After a week part of the outer wall finally collapsed and 2,000 Moslems charged through the breach. As the final hand-to-hand struggle began, the weakened foundations gave way under the weight of the mass of struggling men; the Temple crashed down, burying the last of the Templars and their enemies beneath a smoking pile of rubble. The Holy Land was lost forever, despite the heroic deaths of some 20,000 Templar knights and sergeants since the Order's inception.

The Templars had lands in Cyprus, and it was here that they regrouped to create a new powerbase in the Middle East. But although their great financial network continued to function throughout Europe, the Templars failed to find any realistic military rôle for the future; beyond a few minor and unsuccessful raids on the Syrian and Egyptian coasts, the Order deteriorated into bankers and money-lenders.

This deterioration was seized upon by those who had for many years envied the Order its vast possessions and power, its exemption from royal justice and its overbearing pride. Based on the claim that the Holy Land had been lost by the military orders, who no longer had a purpose for existence

Knight Hospitaller in monastic habit.

since they had failed to take any steps to regain it, a series of attacks was launched against all military orders. Nothing came of these attacks until a renegade Templar, Esquiu de Floyrian, laid specific charges of blasphemy, idolatory and sodomy against the Templars at the court of James II of Aragon. He received a cold reception, but took his accusations to France where Philip the Fair accepted them. The Pope was informed of the charges in 1305, and at the end of the following year the Grand Master, Jacques de Molay, was summoned to Rome. Here the Pope suggested that the Templars and Hospitallers unite to form one order, and that a new crusade be launched from Armenia and Cyprus. De Molay, who had spent all his life as a Templar in the Middle East, seems to have been unaware of the charges levelled against the Order, and failed to see these proposals as a means of saving

the Templars. He rejected both proposals as unworkable. When De Molay returned to Cyprus in 1307, Philip pressed the charges and the Pope agreed to an enquiry. On 15 September Philip sent sealed instructions for the seizure of all members of the Order and their property throughout France. Only 13 Templars escaped the coup; the remainder were thrown into prison, where all except three eventually confessed—under torture—to the charges. The Pope was powerless in the light of the confessions, and on 22 November issued a bull commanding other Christian princes to arrest all Templars in their lands.

Soon, under the agonies of the most atrocious torture, Templars were confessing to homosexuality, devil worship, blasphemy and corruption. Yet for four more years the Order struggled to survive. In England, Spain, Cyprus and Germany the Order was found innocent of the charges; but in France the persecution continued, and scores of Templars who bravely retracted their confessions when the torture ceased were burnt at the stake as heretics. Finally, in April 1312, Philip succeeded in having the Order suppressed; its great wealth was to be passed to the Knights of St John, for the continuation of their hospitaller rôle and their new-found naval operations. It was probably no coincidence that not one penny of the Templars' great wealth in France ever reached the Knights of St John.

The Knights of St John of Jerusalem
After Jerusalem fell to the crusaders its streets were filled with the dead, dying and wounded, and inevitably there followed disease. In about 1070 a group of merchants from the port of Amalfi in Italy had founded the Hospice of St John the Almoner, near the Church of the Holy Sepulchre. A hospice was essentially a place of rest for pilgrims, where they might obtain food and recover from their travels, and it formed a natural part of the main business of the Amalfi merchants—transporting pilgrims to the Holy Land. The hospice was administered by Benedictine monks and nuns from Amalfi, under one Brother Gerard.

Either before or during the siege the hospice had been closed and its staff expelled from the city; but after the siege Brother Gerard reappeared, and the crusaders willingly supported him when he set up a

Knight Hospitaller in military dress—probably early 14th century, to judge from the mixture of mail and plate.

Krak des Chevaliers, gifted to the Hospitallers in 1142, and requiring a garrison of 200 fighting men to hold it.

hospital to care for the sick. The first ruler of Jerusalem, Godfrey of Bouillon, recognised the valuable work of the monks under Gerard by a gift of land, and his example was followed by many others. His successor, Baldwin of Boulogne, also supported the hospital, and when he defeated an Egyptian army he gave one tenth of all the booty to the monks for their good works. This example was copied, and soon the hospital was receiving so much money and land that by 1120, when Gerard died, it had been able to establish a chain of hospices and hospitals throughout the Holy Land.

In 1113 Gerard had abandoned the Benedictine rule for that of St Augustine, and the Hospitallers had been created as an independent religious order by papal bull. Gerard's successor, Raymond du Puy, extended the original work of the new Order until all the main ports of embarkation for pilgrims were equipped with a hospital operated by the Order of St John. However, he also extended the rôle of the Order to the protection of pilgrims on the route from the sea to Jerusalem. The Order's charter included the instruction that it could take up arms in defence of its hospitals, the Order itself, or Jerusalem; but this logical extension of the Order's duties towards pilgrims was to cause a major change in the structure of the Order itself.

In 1126 a Constable of the Order is mentioned, suggesting that there was now some permanent military commitment—possibly involving hired troops, although no details are known. However, there is mention in other documents of 20 monks being detailed to guard the tomb of Christ, and

these became known as the Canons of the Holy Sepulchre ('canon' being an ecclesiastical term originally applicable to all the clergy of any large church). Apparently crusaders also swore obedience to the prior of this body, and took upon themselves the military duties of guarding the tomb. The military members are said to have worn white mantles bearing the red cross of Jerusalem and possibly a white surcoat with a single red cross on it, and to have carried into battle a white banner speckled with red drops to signify the Holy Blood. These were presumably not members of the Order, but were the first knights to volunteer to fight for the Order. The later, true Knights of St John were sometimes referred to as the Knights of the Holy Sepulchre, and when King Alfonso of Aragon and Navarre died in 1134 he left his kingdom to the Hospitallers, the Templars and 'the Canons of the Holy Sepulchre'.

In 1130 the Pope ordained that 'the Religion in war against the Infidel shall bear the standard, with the white cross in a field of red.' Six years later the Order was given the key fortress of Gibelin by the king of Jerusalem; in 1139 Count Raymond II of Tripoli, a confrère of the Hospitallers, bestowed on the Order two of his main castles; and in 1142 the Order received four other castles, including the great Krak des Chevaliers. Such possessions demanded troops to garrison them (Krak des Chevaliers alone required a garrison of 200 knights and sergeants to withstand a siege), but there are no records of the Order being involved in any military rôle at this period. Yet it is inconceivable that the rulers in the Holy Land would have handed over such important fortresses to an organisation incapable of defending them. We know that in 1157 the Order sent a column to relieve the castle of Banyas, and in 1168 it contributed 500 knights to the expedition to Egypt. It has to be assumed that sizeable military forces were available to the Order by at least 1136. By this date there existed the office of Marshal, whose rôle was initially the hiring and control of mercenaries to perform the military duties of the Order, but who commanded the Order's own contingent of 500 knights in 1168. Nur ed-Din, Atabeg of Mosul, considered the Order's soldiers sufficiently formidable to order the execution of those captured in 1157: we cannot now tell whether these were members of the Order, knights holding fiefs with military duties owed to the Order, or mercenaries.

In 1179 a papal bull was issued instructing the Order not to depart from its original objectives; and it was not until after the disastrous battle of Hattin in 1187 that the Pope recognised the need for their military rôle. Even so, he still did nothing to encourage it; and it was not until 1206 that the Order's statutes were revised to provide for military brethren, by which date all the important offices of the Order were in the hands of the soldier-brethren and the Marshal was second in importance only to the Grand Master.

By this date membership of the Order could take several forms. There were brother priests and sisters of St John, who fulfilled the hospitaller duties, and brother knights and sergeants for the military rôle. However, the only recognised division up to 1206 was between priests and lay brethren. Confrère knights were admitted under the same system as described for the Templars. In Europe the houses or 'commanderies' were ruled by commanders, and these were grouped into provinces called 'priories', ruled by priors. By the late 12th century the priories had been collected into larger units called 'grand commanderies', and by the late 13th century these had been grouped into seven 'Langues', or 'tongues'. The hierarchy of the Order resided in the Holy Land and consisted of the Grand Commander of the Order, the Marshal, the Hospitaller, the Treasurer, the Drapier (quartermaster), and the Turcopolier.

Every knight was allowed to own four horses, and he was probably also permitted two esquires, one to lead the spare horses, the other to carry his lance. Both esquires were non-combatant and retired to the rear when action was imminent, where they came under the authority of the Gonfanonier. Sergeants were permitted two horses, and in 1302 they were allowed an esquire. The rank of Military Esquire, presumably commanding the esquires, was an important military office by this date, suggesting that at least some of the esquires may now have had an active military rôle. The sergeants seem to have been fewer in number than the knights, and used less expensive armour.

By the early 13th century the Hospitallers rivalled the Templars as a military power, with perhaps 600 brethren at arms, and clashes between the two Orders became more and more frequent. In 1216 Antioch was captured by the Hospitallers

A 16th-century portrayal of the fall of Acre in 1291, useful for the type of costume and armour likely to have been worn at the sieges of Rhodes (1522) and Malta (1565).

The Hospitaller castle at Bodrum (Halicarnassus) on the west coast of Asia Minor.

from the Templars, but the city rose in revolt, expelled the Hospitallers and confiscated the Order's possessions in that state. By 1240 the diplomatic and political manoeuvres of the two Orders were aimed less against the infidel than against each other. The situation became so bad, with Templars and Hospitallers killing each other in the streets of Acre, that in 1258 a treaty was drawn up to govern the settlement of quarrels between them. But it was already too late.

The decline had begun with the loss of Jerusalem in 1243, and gained speed as the century drew to a close. At Gaza in 1244 over 300 Hospitaller knights and their Master were captured. Over the next 25 years the desperate resistances of isolated garrisons failed to prevent stronghold after stronghold from falling to the Moslems. By 1271 the greatest fortress in the whole of Christendom, the Krak des Chevaliers, had fallen—forced to surrender for lack of sufficient men to defend it. Tripoli fell in 1289; and two years later it was the turn of Acre, called St Jean d'Acre after the magnificent Hospitaller church there. After eight weeks of heroic resistance Acre fell, and the Hospitallers died to a man, fighting alongside their former enemies, the Templars.

Within a year of the fall of Acre the Hospitallers had established new headquarters on their lands in Cyprus, with a castle at Colos and the Hospitaller headquarters at Limassol. The Order had possessed a fleet since the early 13th century, and operations against the infidels were continued in a small way by raids on the mainland. These raids consisted of a landing, the burning of a village or two, and a swift withdrawal.

The king of Cyprus, remembering the great power of the Orders in the Holy Land due to gifts of land there, refused to grant the Hospitallers more land in his kingdom. Unable to grow or to rebuild its former military power, the Order began to look elsewhere for its future. Unlike the Templars, who had resorted to banking, the Hospitallers seem to have realised from their first puny seaborne raids against the Moslems that a military alternative still existed. To survive they must change; and being now an island-based power, they would have to change from a land power to a naval one. The office of Admiral first appears in 1301, in reference to a small fleet raised the previous year. But these would have been mainly transports used for bringing troops, pilgrims and stores to and from the Holy Land. Such vessels would still be required, but so would fighting ships—galleys and galleasses—and it is while the Order was on Cyprus that such ships are first mentioned.

Grand Masters Antony Fluvian de la Rivière, 1421–37 (arms Or, a fess Gules) in monastic habit; and John de Lastia, 1437–54 (arms Gules, a fess Argent) in armour and jupon. Drawings of c.1637 based on contemporary paintings and tapestries at Malta, recently discovered in the Vatican.

Seeking expansion, and seizing on the encroachment of some Moslems on the Byzantine-owned island of Rhodes as an excuse, the Order obtained permission from the Pope to expel the infidel intruders. The first major naval operation from Cyprus was therefore against Rhodes, in 1306. By the end of 1307 the Hospitallers had taken an important stronghold, the fortress of Mount Phileremos, astride the main ridge of mountains and less than ten miles south of the city of Rhodes. Pope Clement V issued a confirmation of the Order's possession of the island in August that year: 'that island . . . which you have taken under your powerful arm, and which today by God's grace you hold, having driven thence the schismatics [the original Christian owners] and completely overthrown the infidel.'

In fact the city of Rhodes was to hold out for another two years, teaching the Hospitallers the great value of the city as a defensible headquarters and costing them their revenues for the next 20 years, against which they obtained a loan from a Venetian money-lender.

This discovery of a new military rôle from their offshore headquarters, and their 'crusade' against the infidels on Rhodes, ensured that when the general reaction set in against the military orders after the loss of the Holy Land, the future of the Hospitallers was not seriously threatened. Instead, the possessions of the suppressed Templars passed into their hands. Even this enormous revenue did not clear their debt, however, for they had undertaken a vast programme of building, constructing massive fortifications on Rhodes as well as building a fleet of warships and colonising several of the islands of the Dodecanese. By 1320 the Hospital owed 500,000 florins to two Italian banking houses. These debts were eventually paid off and a credit established; but in 1343 and 1346 the two banking houses went bankrupt, wiping out the Hospitallers' credit of some 360,000 florins.

Nevertheless, Rhodes and the Order of St John

13

Grand Master Peter d'Aubusson, 1476–1503 (arms Or, a cross moline Gules) receiving Knights Hospitaller in armour and jupons. Note mail protection for upper arms and torso, popular in Italy—and perhaps in Rhodes—in the late 15th century because it was cooler to wear than plate.

were now exceedingly strong, the island being fortified and garrisoned by about 400 knights. Freed from the internal politics which had hampered it since the military branch was formed, and operating in a theatre where they were the sole major power, the Order set about the destruction of the Moslem corsairs who dominated the eastern Mediterranean. To further stabilise the Order, it was reorganised in 1331 with the knights of the various nationalities grouped in national Langues, the balance of power being guaranteed by allocating certain offices to each Langue.

In 1345 the Hospitallers had their first significant victory since the capture of Rhodes. The island of Smyrna had been occupied by the Emir of Aydin in 1328, and from this island the emir's fleet raided as far as Greece, disrupting Christian trade. The Hospitallers contributed six galleys to a papal force which attacked the island in 1345, and were eventually entrusted with the control of the port

there. Smyrna remained an important naval base for Christian forces until it fell to the Mongols in 1402.

In 1365 a 'crusade' was launched by the Cypriots under Pierre I de Lusignan, and was supported by the Hospitallers. After an initial success at Alexandria, the crusade degenerated into an orgy of looting and destruction. New crusades were launched in 1390 and 1396 but the Order's rôle in these was limited to small contingents of galleys—for by now the Order had evolved into a completely naval power, their attempts to expand their territory beyond the island of Rhodes having failed. Henceforth they were totally preoccupied with the destruction of Turkish shipping along the coast of Asia Minor.

As the other Christian powers in the eastern Mediterranean declined and disappeared, so the attention of the Egyptian and Ottoman sultans began to turn towards the Hospitallers. In 1435 the sultan of Egypt, having reduced Cyprus to a vassal state, began to prepare a move against Rhodes. Reinforcements of 500 knights were recruited from the West, and in 1440 the first attack by a squadron of Egyptian galleys was decisively defeated. In 1444 a much larger naval force appeared off the island, a vast army of mamluks was successfully landed and the island completely overrun. The city of Rhodes was besieged for over a month before the Egyptians were finally driven off by a daring counter-attack, and the invasion was abandoned.

When Constantinople fell in 1453, Rhodes became the last outpost of Christianity in the East. The Ottoman sultan Mohammad II demanded tribute from Rhodes, and received a curt refusal. In 1480 he arrived with a great fleet to subdue the island. After three months of siege work and three major assaults on the city's defences, the arrival of relief ships enabled the Hospitallers to drive off their attackers.

The final attack on the Hospitallers' stronghold was launched in 1522 by the sultan Suleiman. The Order's Grand Master, Villiers de l'Isle Adam, had 600 Hospitallers and about 4,500 local auxiliaries against a Turkish army of some 100,000 men. However, Rhodes was one of the greatest fortresses in the world, equipped with excellent artillery batteries, and it took Suleiman two months of siege operations to effect a breach in the walls at the weakest point—the landward side, garrisoned by the Langues of Aragon and England. Over the next three weeks three major assaults were made on the breach by fanatical Moslem troops, exhibiting a religious fervour to match that which had enabled the Christian crusaders to conquer the Holy Land nearly 300 years earlier. All three assaults were beaten off, though not without considerable loss to the garrison. Suleiman now dismissed his commander and appointed in his place an engineer. Costly assaults were replaced by a war of attrition, with the island sealed off from reinforcements and supplies by a complete blockade. By 20 December 1522 the Hospitallers were faced with two alternatives: total extermination, or surrender. Suleiman's terms were generous, and were accepted. After 200 years the Order was again homeless.

The Emperor Charles V resettled the Order on the strategic island of Malta on condition that it also defended Tripoli in North Africa. This was an impossible task, but fortunately the liability ended when Tripoli was taken by the Turks in 1551 after a gallant struggle by the Hospitaller garrison. In the meantime the Order had converted Malta into a great fortress surpassing even its previous headquarters, and was now busily engaged in fighting the corsairs of the Barbary coast, centred on Algeria. The corsairs had been seriously hampering all Mediterranean trade, and even carried out raids into Italy and Spain; but 200 years of naval warfare had created a Christian force more than the equal of the corsairs. Soon the names of the Hospitaller captains were as feared amongst the Moslems as the

The siege of Rhodes in 1480, showing the attack on the south-east corner of the walls. The brethren of the Order of St John are wearing red surcoats with the Order's white cross.

corsair captains had been amongst the Christians.

In 1565 Suleiman arrived off Malta with a fleet of 180 ships and about 30,000 men. The great siege of Malta was about to begin. Reinforced by knights from every commandery in Europe, the Hospitallers settled down in their spacious and well-supplied fortress to endure the last and most famous siege of their long history. There were about 500 knights of the Order on the island, supported by 4,000 Maltese levies and some 4,500 other troops, including mercenaries. Another 80 knights and 600 other troops managed to slip through the blockade later, but Suleiman's original force was doubled in strength as the siege dragged on.

The initial attack was made at the end of May on the fort of St Elmo, guarding the entrance to the Grand Harbour. After a month of fierce fighting the fort finally fell; the survivors of the heroic garrison were slaughtered, and their mutilated bodies were floated across the harbour. The Hospitallers

Detail of the walls of Rhodes in 1522.

retaliated by executing the prisoners they held, and firing their heads into the enemy camp. Thereafter the siege became a grim struggle to the death, with no quarter given by either side.

On 15 July 1565 a general assault was launched by land and sea. It very nearly succeeded. A breach was created by mining on 7 August, and again the Turks came dangerously close to success. On the

Sketch of the port of Malta in 1565, showing the various defences and the siege works and camps of Suleiman.

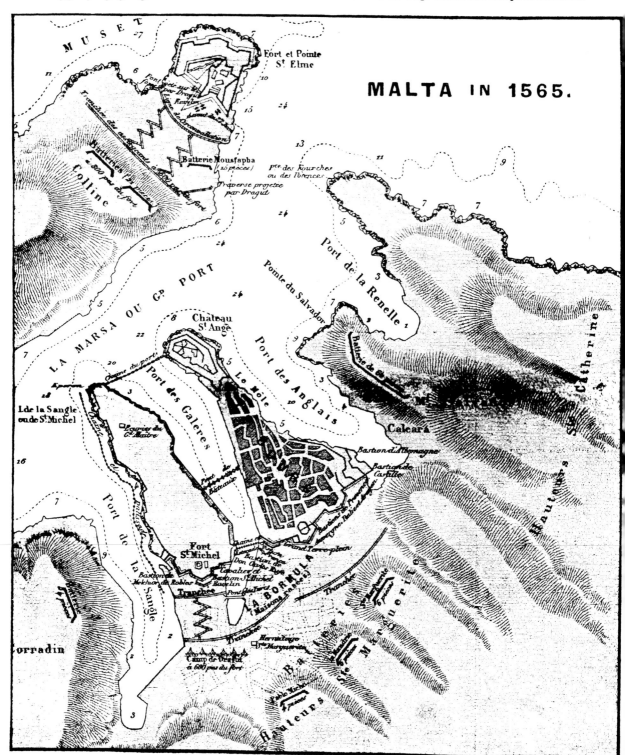

19th and 23rd two more great assaults were launched, but by now the Hospitallers had repaired the breaches, and both assaults were beaten off. On 7 September a Spanish army arrived to relieve the garrison; the dispirited Turkish army was allowed to embark and sail away unmolested, having suffered some 24,000 casualties. The Hospitallers had lost 240 knights and some 6,000 other troops.

The weakening of Turkish naval power at Lepanto in 1571, and the lack of a leader of Suleiman's calibre in succeeding years, led to the Order becoming more and more preoccupied with its commercial interests as the need for its military rôle declined. The fortresses were slowly turned into palaces, and in the 17th century dissension began to arise between the Spanish and French Langues. Yet the final blow did not fall until the French Revolution, when the Order's estates in Europe were seized. Deprived of revenues, divided amongst themselves, resented by the tax-burdened Maltese, and lacking a strong leader, the Order finally surrendered Malta to Napoleon in 1798 after a siege lasting only two days.

The Knights of St Lazarus

This was the third military order to develop in Jerusalem, and is believed to have had its origins in a leper hospital run by Greeks and Armenians before the First Crusade. It was probably founded as the separate Order of St Lazarus in the second decade of the 12th century, although the earliest mention is *circa* 1130, when the Hospital of Lepers, built on the outer face of the northern wall of Jerusalem, was taken over by Frankish hospitallers who followed the Augustinian rule. These were

16th-century breastplates belonging to Knights Hospitaller and bearing the cross of the Order.

Turkish cannon balls of marble, used during the 1480 and 1522 sieges of Rhodes.

possibly members of the Order of St John, for tradition holds that the first Master of the Hospitallers was also the first Master of the St Lazarus Order. Certainly the rules of both Templars and Hospitallers stated that a knight who caught leprosy must leave the Order and join the brethren of St Lazarus, who wore a black habit without insignia.

The new Order had its own church and convent by 1142, and by 1147 was known as the Leper Brothers of Jerusalem. By 1155 the Order had houses in Tiberias and Ascalon, and later in Acre and possibly Caesarea and Beirut. By the mid-12th century the Order had also developed a force of military brethren, but they were never very numerous, and the Order remained principally preoccupied with the hospitaller rôle. A few non-leper brethren were included in the Order as knights, and leprous knights almost certainly took up arms when necessary. There were also lay brethren-sergeants, recruited from commoners suffering from leprosy.

A detachment of the Order may have fought at Hattin in 1187. We know that there was certainly a contingent at the disastrous battle of Gaza in 1244, where the Order suffered heavy losses. When Jerusalem fell in 1243 the Order moved its headquarters to Acre, where it had its Tower of Lazarus in the northern suburb of Montmusard, and was responsible for the defence of that area. In 1253 the Order made an ill-fated foray against the Moslems in Ramleh, and was saved from utter destruction only by the intervention of Louis IX of

Alberto Aringhieri, a knight of St John, shown in monastic habit in a fresco painted (*c*.1503–08) by Pinturicchio in Siena Cathedral. The walls of Rhodes are illustrated in the background of the painting.

France. The military brethren fought in the defence of Acre in 1291, where all those present were killed.

The Order moved to Cyprus after the fall of Acre, but soon abandoned its military activities. It carried on its hospitaller rôle until about 1342, and continued a shadowy existence from then until the late Renaissance when it was revived in Savoy and France. The French branch—The Order of Our Lady of Mount Carmel and St Lazarus—was cultivated by Louis XIV as a rival to the Order of St John, and by 1696 the Order had over 140 commanderies and maintained a small squadron of warships to 'fight the English pirates'. These latter-day knights wore a white tunic embroidered with an orange and green cross. The Order was finally suppressed in 1790.

The Hospitallers of St Thomas of Canterbury in Acre

When the crusaders besieged Acre in 1189–91, the chaplain of the Dean of St Paul's in England began to nurse the sick and wounded in the besiegers' camp. After the capture of the city he built a small chapel, funded by Richard I, and founded a hospital with nursing brethren for the care of Englishmen. The Order, which followed the Cistercian rule and became known as the Knights of St Thomas Acon, soon acquired lands in Cyprus, Sicily, Naples, and later Greece; and a headquarters was set up in London at the birthplace of Thomas à Becket, now the site of the Mercers' Hall, the Mercers of the City of London having been patrons of the Order from as early as 1190. In 1231 the Bishop of Winchester bequeathed the Order a large sum of money and encouraged it to follow the example of the Templars, although the Order always maintained its hospitaller rôle.

The Order was always small, most Englishmen preferring to join the Hospitallers; but nine knights and the Master fought at Acre in 1291, where they all died. The Order then declined, although it maintained a commandery in Cyprus during the 14th century. The last known knight of the Order was Frater Richard de Tickhill, knighted in 1357 at the church of St Nicholas of the English in Nicosia.

According to Seward the knights wore a white mantle bearing a red cross on which was a white scallop shell—the traditional badge of pilgrims. The Victoria County History for Surrey (vol. IV p. 26) argues a more convincing case for a black mantle (as would be expected of a Cistercian order) with a 'cross formy per pale argent and gules'. In 1236 Pope Gregory IX gave members of the Order permission to wear a half-red, half-white cross, divided vertically, so that they might be distinguished from the Templars.

The German Orders

The Teutonic Knights

During the Fourth Crusade, at the siege of Acre in 1190, a group of German merchants from Bremen and Lübeck set up a tented hospital on the shore before the city to tend the many wounded and sick crusaders from the large German contingent. Such a step was not unusual, and similar ethnic establishments had been founded over the years for various groups of crusaders who could not speak French, including Hungarians and oriental Christians.

The siege of Acre lasted eight months, and by its end the temporary hospital had become a permanent institution. The financial support of

Frederick of Schwaben and his royal brother Henry VI enabled the hospitallers to create a new hospital within the city walls. By 1196 the hospitallers had several branches in the Christian lands, and had been officially recognised by the Pope as an independent (though rather small) Order, following the rule of the Order of St John.

The following year a large contingent of German knights arrived in the Holy Land. The earliest chronicle of the Order, *Die Statuten des Deutschen Ordens*, written some years later, describes what happened next:

'To many of the German princes it seemed useful and noble to bestow on the hospital the Rule of the Templars. For this purpose the German prelates, princes and nobles assembled in the house of the Templars [in Acre] and invited to such a salutary gathering some of the available prelates and barons of the Holy Land. One and all decided unanimously that the hospital should follow in regard to the poor and the sick the Rule of the Hospital of St John in Jerusalem as it had done until now; whereas in regard to clergy, knights and other brothers, it should follow henceforth the Rule of the Templars. After this decision was taken the prelates and the masters of the Templars presented the new house with the Rule of the Temple and then they elected there a brother of the house, Henry surnamed Walpoto, as master. The master of the Temple handed to him the written Rule of the Knights of the Temple which henceforth had to be followed in the house.'

By February 1199 Pope Innocent had granted the new military Order official recognition. By 1220 the Order had 12 houses in Palestine, Greece, southern Italy and Germany. Under the High Master (Hochmeister) Herman von Salza, many rich gifts were lavished on the Order until it was in a position to finance its own crusade, and by about 1230 was capable of fielding some 600 military brethren. However, in the Holy Land itself all the important castles and lands had already been granted to the Hospitallers and Templars, and the Teutonic Order there remained small and poor in consequence, having to buy almost all its lands.

Initially the Order concentrated on Antioch and Tripoli, but in the campaign of 1216 the

Knight of St John in armour and jupon, as painted by Pinturicchio in the fresco in Siena Cathedral.

Hochmeister and most of the Order's military brethren were killed. A new headquarters was built north-east of Acre, the castle of Starkenberg, and the Order continued to participate in all the major military events of the 13th century; but the Teutonic Knights were never able to become a powerful military or political force in the Holy Land, and thus never became involved in its disastrous political intrigues.

The Teutonic Order had always maintained a distinct national identity, and this, together with its inability to expand in the Holy Land, had inevitably caused it to develop a special connection with Germany. Soon after Von Salza became Hochmeister in 1210, King Andrew of Hungary requested the help of the Order against marauding bands of Kumans who were ravaging the province of Transylvania. In return for their help, the king promised the Order the district of Burzenland. The Teutonic Order undertook this 'crusade' at their own expense, and by 1225 had pacified the province and begun to settle Burzenland with German colonists. An alarmed King Andrew ordered their eviction. The Order was not powerful enough to hold their newly won land against the king, and had to withdraw; but the campaign had

Galleon of the Grand Master of St John at Malta. The sails and various insignia were in the red and white of the Order, the hull black with gilt decoration.

turned its attention towards Eastern Europe.

Church missions had been active in Prussia since the 10th century, but the resistance of the Prussians to conversion had seemed to increase in proportion to the pressure put on them, and in 1217 the bishop had had to call for crusaders to protect his converts. The first Prussian crusade was launched in 1221. This provoked a massive retaliation, and by 1224 the Polish Duke Conrad of Masovia was asking the Teutonic Knights for help.

Herman von Salza was not prepared to venture into what would be virtually a new crusade until he had obtained full approval from both the German emperor and the Pope. Nor was he willing to risk the future of the Order without some guarantee that he would not be betrayed again. Negotiations on these points dragged on for some years.

In 1226 the Emperor Frederick II paid the Order a great honour by making the Hochmeister and all his successors princes of the German Empire, with the right to display the imperial eagle on their arms as representatives of the Holy Roman Empire in the struggle to win new lands and converts. When Frederick was crowned king of Jerusalem in 1229, it was the Teutonic Order which provided the guard of honour in the Holy Sepulchre.

By 1229 the Duke of Masovia had been compelled to surrender all rights to the Kulm province on the Vistula, south of Gdansk; and both the Pope and the emperor agreed that the land of the heathen tribes, the Prusiskai, should be held fully and freely by the Order, with only nominal papal suzerainty. Von Salza now had a secure base for a Prussian crusade.

A base for initial operations had already been established by the building of a castle at Vogelsang on the Elbe in 1228, and in 1230 20 knights and 200 sergeants of the Teutonic Order, commanded by Frater Hermann Balke, began the pacification of the Kulm province. The fighting was ferocious and merciless, fought over an almost impenetrable wilderness of sand dunes, lakes, rivers, bogs and dense dark forests along the shores of the Baltic. In this gloomy and mysterious world of the heathen tribes ambushes were the normal way of fighting, and prisoners were subjected to frightful tortures in pagan rites.

Over the next two years the tiny force of Teutonic knights and sergeants systematically reduced all organised resistance, building fortresses as they advanced, burning every village they encountered, and exterminating every man, woman and child who would not accept Christianity. The great castle of Kulm was built in 1232, Marienwerder in 1233, Thorn in 1234, and Elbing in 1237. More and more natives submitted to the new religion, becoming serfs of the Order, and sometimes allies in a bitter war against former rivals. By 1239 the Order had reached the coast, and had established a network of fortresses from which they could dominate the whole territory.

Hermann Balke was now ordered to continue his work in Livonia with 60 knights, and at this time the Order became divided into three distinct branches: the German branch, which was concentrated mainly in south and south-western Germany, including Alsace and possessions in Burgundy; a

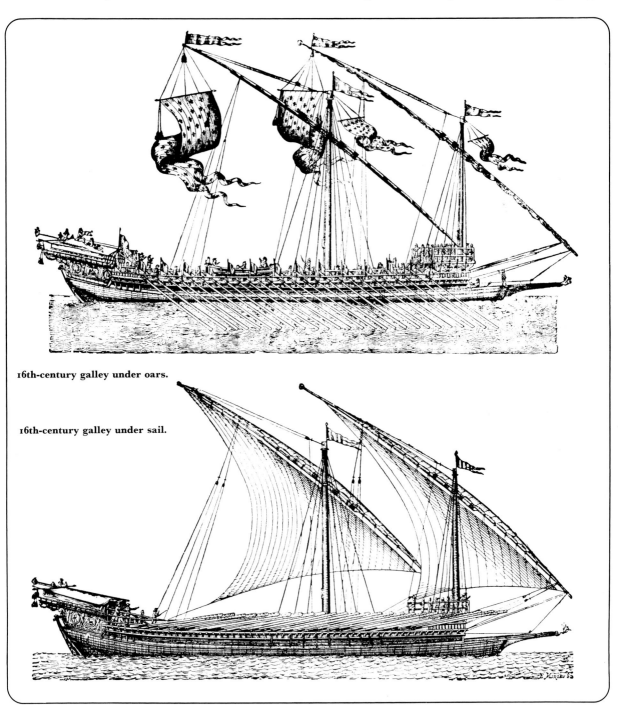

16th-century galley under oars.

16th-century galley under sail.

Prussian branch in the newly conquered territory, with its centre at Marienburg and its own province commander, called a Landmeister; and the 'new' province of Livonia, originally pacified by the Brethren of the Sword (see below), and of which Balke was made Landmeister. However, although the Order was now centred in Prussia, it maintained its rôle in the Holy Land, and the Hochmeisters normally lived in Acre, so the headquarters of the Order could be said to have remained there.

Each province was divided into houses or *Komtureis*, each of 12 brothers commanded by a *Komtur*. Smaller territorial sub-divisions were headed by *Vogts* or caretakers. Below the *Hochmeister* were the officers of the central administration of the Order: the *Gross Komtur*, *Ordensmarschall* or *Grossmarschall*, *Spittler* (Hospitaller), *Tressler* (Treasurer), and *Trapier* (quartermaster).

17th-century galleasse.

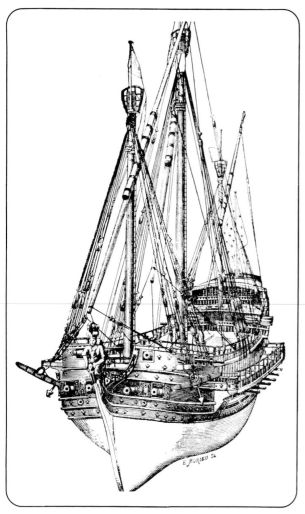

In 1242 the Livonian brethren tried to enlarge their province at the expense of other Christians— the Russians of the Eastern Church—and an expeditionary force crossed the River Narva and headed towards Novgorod. The Order was met by a Russian army led by Prince Alexander Nevsky, and was brought to battle on the frozen Lake Peipus. The ice broke under the weight of the armour and horses of the knights, and most perished by drowning, or at the hands of the lighter Russian cavalry. (This defeat, which effectively stopped the Order's expansion northwards, was immortalised in Eisenstein's classic film *Alexander Nevsky*.)

In the same fateful year there was a great Prussian uprising, organised by Svantepolle of Pomerania, a former ally of the Order. The uprising reversed most of the progress made by the Prussian brethren over the past 12 years; some of the smaller castles were lost, and it took them seven years to suppress the Prussians once again.

The Livonian and Prussian brethren then set out to conquer the coastal lands which divided them— Samland and Courland. A great crusade in 1253 led to the founding of Königsberg, and a series of military and political successes led to the total occupation of Samland by 1260. But in that same year the natives, by a series of lucky accidents, managed to kill a great number of the Order at the battle of Durben. The neighbouring Lithuanians at once repudiated their alliance with the Order; the Prussian tribes rebelled again; and 20 years' work was undone almost overnight. Only massive help from outside (the Pope issued 22 bulls calling for crusaders between 1261 and 1264) saved the Order. By 1272 the tide had begun to turn once more; the strength of the Order grew again, until by the late 1270s it could field 2,000 military brethren, and by 1290 the last vestiges of rebellion had been crushed. But by this date the great age of crusading zeal, of conquest and conversion, was over.

In the Holy Land the castle of Starkenberg had been lost in 1271, and with the fall of Acre in 1291 the Teutonic Knights moved their headquarters to Venice. In 1308, by which date it had become obvious that there was no longer any hope of regaining a foothold in the Holy Land, an attempt was made to suppress the Order on the grounds of cruelty and witchcraft.

Similar accusations, inspired by the persecution

Armour worn by Vincenzo Capponi (1545–70), a knight of Malta, who fought in the siege of 1565. (Courtesy the Capponi Collection)

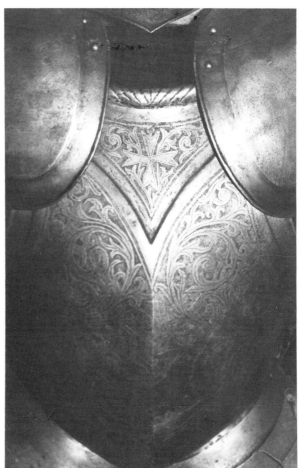

Detail of the Order's cross on the breastplate of the Capponi armour. (Courtesy the Capponi Collection)

of the Templars, were levelled against other military orders in an attempt to find a scapegoat for the loss of the Holy Land. The Teutonic Order solved the problem by concentrating its efforts and offices in its eastern lands, where crusades could still be carried out with official blessing, and where the Order was secure in the remote vastness of its own territories. In September 1309 the Hochmeister and other leading officers of the Order entered Marienburg, henceforth to be the headquarters of the Order. The office of the Prussian Landmeister was taken over by the Hochmeister.

In about 1310 the kingdom of Lithuania was revived under the leadership of Gedymin, and from then onwards the Lithuanian kings were the chief enemies of the Order, being not only the last heathens in the region but also actively pursuing a course of conquest. In the first three-quarters of the 14th century the Order launched some 80 expeditions against the Lithuanians, sometimes waging as many as eight campaigns in one year. These were fought over terrain similar to that of Prussia: swamps, dense forests, sand dunes, rivers and lakes. Often unable to act as cavalry because of the dreadful terrain, the knights marched on foot through the gloomy forests, or used boats and rafts to carry them across the lakes and misty swamps. The Order's military reputation reached its peak during this period, and for generations the highest praise that could be given to a Christian nobleman was that he had become a knight in Prussia. The greatest and noblest knights of the age, such as the Frenchman Jean Boucicaut, rode with the Order against the Lithuanian pagans, as did Henry Bolingbroke (Earl of Derby and later Henry IV of England), King Louis of Hungary, and King John of Bohemia.

However, the expansion and great strength of the Order created jealous enemies. The two great Catholic monarchies of eastern Europe, Poland and Hungary, allied themselves in an attempt to curtail the power of the Order; but their intrigues with the Lithuanians had little effect until 1380, when the Grand Duke of Lithuania married the queen-regnant of Poland. In one stroke the Poles had accomplished by diplomacy what 75 years of campaigning by the Order had failed to achieve—for the terms of the marriage settlement included the acceptance of Christianity by the Lithuanian people.

With its official *raison d'être* removed, the Order inevitably began to decline. By 1400 the number of military brethren had fallen to 1,600. Meddling in the internal power struggles of the new Polish-Lithuanian state did not endear them to their former enemies, and soon a series of allegiances and treacheries led to a number of skirmishes and eventually to war.

Jagiello (Ladislos II) of Lithuania mobilised an army of about 10,000 troops, including all the

Effigy of Don Juan Ruiz de Vergara, Proctor of the Langue of Castile from 1575, from his tomb in the old cathedral of Valladolid. Note very large eight-pointed cross of the Order on his breast: this was the size of cross preferred in the Order in the mid-15th to 16th centuries.

enemies of the Order—Poles, Lithuanians, Russians, Bohemians (under Ziska), Hungarians and even Tartars and Cossacks—and invaded the Order's territory in July 1410. The Hochmeister decided to strike as quickly as possible, without waiting for the Livonian brethren, and immediately marched towards the enemy. The two armies met on the wooded, rolling hills of the Grunwald, or Tannenberg. Jagiello's army was encamped in the forest itself, thus denying the Order its strongest tactic—the mounted charge of its knights. The Hochmeister therefore deployed for a defensive engagement and waited for the enemy to attack, relying on his numerous crossbowmen and archers to halt any assault.

When the allied army began its attack the Order's crossbowmen and archers did succeed in putting to flight the Lithuanians on one wing, but the centre and the other wing came on, and a major struggle ensued. The triumphant pursuers of the Lithuanians were checked by Russian cavalry and a Polish reserve, and for some time there was no advantage to either side. Then the Hochmeister led his remaining reserve in an attempt to pierce the Polish line. He failed; he and the other leading officers of the Order were surrounded and killed, and after a brief struggle the rest of his army broke

1: Knight Hospitaller, 12th-13th C
2: Turcopole, 12th-13th C
3: Foot soldier, 12th-13th C

A

1: Knight Templar, c.1150
2: Pilgrim, 12th-14th C
3: Knight Templar, late 13th C

B

1: Teutonic Knight, c.1230
2: Teutonic Knight, c.1300
3: Sergeant, Teutonic Order,
   c.1230

C

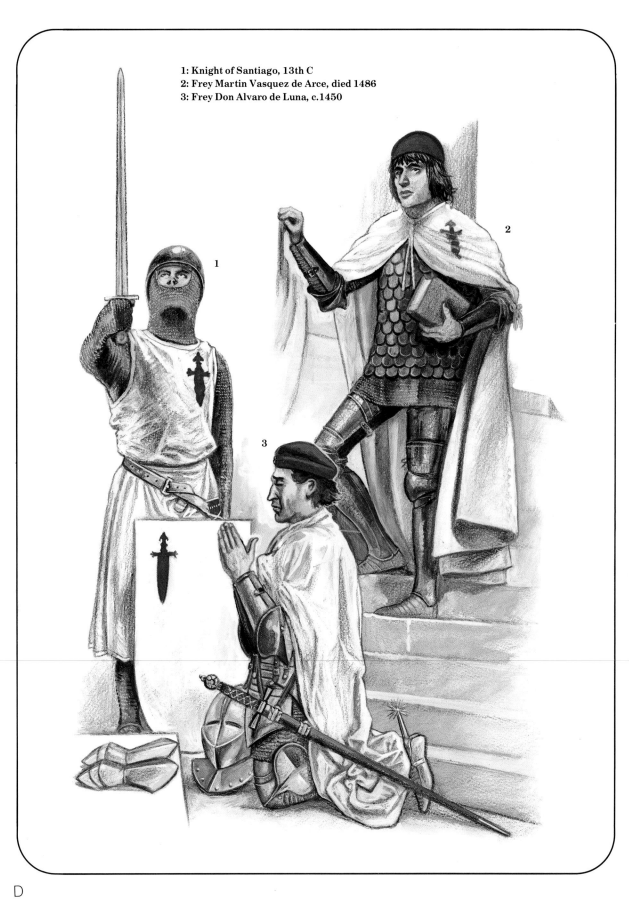

1: Knight of Santiago, 13th C
2: Frey Martin Vasquez de Arce, died 1486
3: Frey Don Alvaro de Luna, c.1450

D

1: Knight Hospitaller, early 14th C
2: Knight Hospitaller, c. 1530
3: Knight Hospitaller, mid-16th C

E

1: Hochmeister of the Teutonic Order,
   mid-15th C
2: Fra Petrus von Düsburg, c.1330
3: Fra Kuno von Liebensteyn,
   died 1391

F

Master and two knights of
the Order of St John, 1480

G

1: Sir Thomas Docwra, c.1515
2: Philip de l'Isle Adam, c.1525
3: Knight of Malta (St John), 17th C

and fled, leaving some 200 of the Order's knights dead on the field. Many others were captured and subsequently tortured and beheaded.

The Order never recovered its former military strength, and was compelled to avoid outright battle in the wars which followed, concluding disadvantageous peace agreements in both 1422 and 1435. Marienburg had to be abandoned in 1457, and in 1466 West Prussia was surrendered to the Polish king. The Order moved its headquarters to Königsberg. The decline continued, and in 1525 the Hochmeister had to sign the Treaty of Cracow, whereby Prussia was henceforth held only as a hereditary duchy from the king of Poland.

The Order fought for the Emperor Charles V during the religious wars of the Schmalkaldic League, 1546–47, and the Landmeister of Livonia remained independent until 1559–60, when Ivan the Terrible invaded the province with an army of 130,000 men. Now 2,000 strong, the Order was also confronted by a rising of the Estonian peasantry. Fortress after fortress fell. At Weissenstein in 1562 a force of only 2,000 men managed to beat off a Russian army of 30,000; but the *Ordensland* was

falling apart. The Swedes occupied northern Estonia, the Danes seized the offshore islands, and the Landmeister was forced to cede all the Order's territories in Poland.

The Order survived in Germany, and even more so in Austria, under a master now called the Hoch-und-Deutschmeister. At the siege of Vienna in 1683 the Order was able to provide a full regiment, which proved a mainstay of the defence; and from 1695 the Order's revenues were used to finance the Hoch-und-Deutschmeister Regiment in the fight against the Turks. The Order's last great battle was at Zenta in 1697, when Prince Eugene of Savoy practically annihilated a major Turkish invasion of Hungary—the last serious Turkish threat to that country.

The Austrian Hoch-und-Deutschmeister Regiment survived to fight in both World Wars, but the only real military rôle played by the Order itself after 1697 lay in the individual prowess of its officers, now limited to 20 nobles who were always officers in the German Army. These included men

Malta in the time of Grand Master Vilhena, 1722–36.

25

The lands invaded and occupied by the Teutonic Order.

such as the master Archduke Karl, Napoleon's great adversary; Count Maximilian von Merveldt, who fought against the French in the Revolutionary and Napoleonic Wars with great distinction; the Master Archduke Eugen, who played an important part in the victory of Caporetto in 1917; and, perhaps, the 12 brethren who were hanged in July 1944 after the plot to assassinate Hitler had failed.

The Brethren of the Sword

Cistercian missionaries had been active in Livonia from about 1150, but despite a crusade in 1171–76 the Church was unable to make any real progress in the province. In 1201 Albrecht von Buxhövden led a large expedition which proved successful, and was able to found the city of Riga. Buxhövden was made bishop of Riga, and either he or his colonists founded in about 1202 a military order, *Fratres Militiae Christi*, for the defence of the colony. A Cistercian order, the knights came to be known as the Brethren of the Sword both from their military rôle and from the sword badge worn on their clothing.

In their first year there were perhaps only ten knights, but within two years this number had increased to 50, with 100 serving brothers, and fortresses established at Wenden and Fellin. Most of the knights came from a small area of central Germany.

Although eventually possessing 13 commanderies, the Order was never able to build up that network of rich possessions and powerful patrons which would have enabled them to become a strong military and political power, able to survive even the worst setbacks. Almost all the Order's lands lay in newly conquered territory, one-third of which was always given to them for their services, and therefore the revenues from these lands were rarely large. Moreover, any military defeat usually resulted in the loss of these lands, and the loss of revenue from them, as well as the deaths of knights who were difficult to replace.

Nevertheless, for the first ten years the Order was successful, and its only real setbacks were the rebellions of 1212 in Latvia and of 1223 in Estonia, when a third of the Order's members were slain. By 1226 the Order was in control of two-thirds of Livonia.

A new crusading army arrived at Riga in September 1236. The Hochmeister, knowing the country and the enemy, advised the newcomers to wait for winter. This must have seemed strange advice to men accustomed to campaigning in spring and summer, but in this part of Europe campaigns were normally fought in the winter because only then were the marshes made passable by freezing over. The crusaders rejected the advice, and the Hochmeister was honour bound to support their campaign. Inevitably the crusaders were ambushed, and trapped on a marshy island at Siauliai in Courland by the Lithuanians. Deprived of their most effective weapon—the mounted charge—the crusaders suffered a severe defeat in which half the Sword Brethren perished.

Surviving members of the Order, together with the remaining lands in Courland and Estonia, were amalgamated with the Teutonic Order in 1237–39 under the first Landmeister of Livonia, Hermann Balke. Even so, the brethren managed to maintain their separate identity, aided by the isolation of the Livonian province; and until comparatively recently historians believed that the two Orders had remained separate due to the independent actions and survival of the Livonian branch after Tannenburg.

Spanish Military Orders

Military orders appeared rather late in Spain, considering that the *reconquista* began in the 11th century, but nevertheless their contingents added a vital and powerful core of professional troops to the crusader armies of Spain and Portugal.

The Hospitallers acquired their first foothold in

Conrad of Thuringia, Grand Master of the Teutonic Order 1239–41, from his tombstone.

Catalonia in 1143, and the Templars were well established in Spain by 1146. Both were generously supported by the Spanish kings, who anticipated military aid by way of return. But neither of these two great Orders was willing to commit itself to the wars in Spain: they saw their major rôle in the Holy Land, and it was for this reason that eventually the purely Spanish and Portuguese military orders arose.

It is thought that the earliest of these 'Orders' were no more than associations of knights defending small frontier stations—*ribats*. Such brotherhoods of knights were not uncommon, as we have seen in the Holy Land, but usually they were of a temporary nature. The first such brotherhood of knights to become established as a permanent force in Spain was that known as:

The Knights of Calatrava

The Templars had been granted the royal fortress of Calatrava, on what was then the frontier with Islam, in 1147. Ten years later they abandoned it on the grounds that it was indefensible, leaving the road to Toledo wide open to attack. In desperation, Sancho of Castile offered the fortress to anyone who was prepared to hold it, with sufficient territory to maintain the costs of its defence. A Cistercian abbot from Navarre, Ramón Sierra of Fitero, came forward; and he and his monks were transferred to Calatrava, where they were joined by many Navarrese soldiers. By the end of 1158 they had cleared the region of raiders.

When Ramón died in 1164 the monks returned to Fitero, leaving the castle to be held by the knights. The new master, Don Garcia, swore to observe the Cistercian rule; priests were recruited to serve as chaplains, and that same year the Order was recognised by the Pope.

In 1179 a commandery was founded at Alcañiz in Aragon to fight the Moors of Valencia, and this later became one of the Order's greatest houses. In 1195, at the battle of Alarcos, King Alfonso VIII of Castile was defeated by the Moors; some 25,000 Castillians were killed or captured, among them many of the brethren of Calatrava. The Moors advanced slowly northwards, and within two years Calatrava itself had been lost. A new headquarters was set up at Salvatierra, and the knights now called themselves the Knights of Salvatierra.

The Teutonic Order's commandery at Rheden, West Prussia, as it appeared in the late 13th century.

This headquarters also had to be evacuated in 1211, but in the following year Calatrava was retaken. The Masters of the Order then concentrated on the Order's position in Castile, disposing of their lands in the other kingdoms, until the Order was in control of Castile from Toledo to the Sierra Nevada. Headquarters were then moved to Calatrava la Nueva in the Sierra de Atalayo, as the original fortress at Calatrava had lost its strategic importance. The Order was now one of the most wealthy and powerful bodies in the kingdom, providing its only standing army, and this created conflict with the king. From 1254 the king took part in the election of the Order's officers, and by 1476 the crown had begun to control the Order. When the Master died in 1487, no new Master was appointed. By 1494 members of the Order were allowed to marry, and it had lost both its original form and its original purpose.

Members of the Order originally wore a hooded white mantle, that of the *caballeros* being shortened for riding. On active service a long sleeveless surcoat was worn, and sometimes a fur-lined cloak. There was no insignia, but the knights' armour was always black. In 1397 the Order adopted a red cross insignia—originally a cross fleury, but the 'leaves' of the fleur-de-lis were later bent back until they touched the 'stem' to form an M for 'Maria', i.e. more like a cross flory. From about 1400 onwards the knights wore a short dark grey or black tunic with the red cross on the left breast, but all brethren still wore the white mantle in the cloisters.

The Knights of Santiago

Some time after 1158, when the Moorish threat was at its height, a small band of 13 knights operating near Cáceres in Castile offered their services to the Canons of St Eloi in Léon for the protection of pilgrims travelling to the shrine of St James at Compostella. In about 1164 these Knights of Cáceres were given the Castillian frontier town of Uclés to defend. By 1171 there were clerics as well as

Marienburg (now Malbork Castle) beside the River Nogat in Poland, built _c._1276 and headquarters of the Teutonic Order from 1309. This magnificent building was restored in the 19th century, but reduced to ruins during the Second World War.

knights following the Augustinian rule, and in 1175 the brotherhood was recognised by the Pope as a new Order. The rule was adapted from those of St Augustine and the Templars, with the lay brethren divided into knights and foot soldiers, and the Order was governed by a Master and a council, under the general supervision of the Pope.

The Knights of Santiago were the most unorthodox of the religious military orders in that they were, strictly speaking, not a monastic order. Although the brethren lived in communities in their castles and were inspired by religious fervour, the knights were allowed to marry and to have personal possessions—cancelling two of the three monastic vows. This seems to have been a special privilege granted by the Pope. However, on the death of a knight all his wealth was inherited by the Order, which then became responsible for the care of his family. The Order's prime rôle was always the military one, and its knights rendered valuable service in the unceasing frontier wars of the Order's early years—their commitment extending so far as to ignore royal truces with the Moors, which they did not recognise as binding on their Order.

The Order grew rapidly in the next decade, and acquired lands in France, Italy, Palestine, Hungary and England. Headquarters were established at Montalban in Aragon. Among the Order's acquisitions was a castle at Palmela in Portugal, which became a commandery (_encomienda_) and recruited Portuguese knights. By 1287 the knights at this _encomienda_ had formed themselves into a separate Order, Sao Thiago, with their own Master, although their independent identity was not recognised by the Pope until 1317.

By the mid-13th century the Order's fame was such that it was promised large lands in Asia Minor if it could send knights to fight for Baldwin of Constantinople, but the Order was not numerous enough to take up the offer. By this date the Order insisted on noble birth for anyone wishing to enter as a knight: this increase in nobility within the Order led to a much closer connection with the royal court, and a corresponding increase in royal interest in its activities. From 1254 the king expected to have a say in the election of officers, and by 1275 he was promoting his own favourites to the post of Master. In 1342 the king's gift of the mastership to his seven-year-old bastard led to protests from, amongst others, the Master of Alcantara, who was besieged in his castle and beheaded. Shortly afterwards the Master of Calatrava was assassinated by Pedro the Cruel for plotting against the king's favourite.

The last flowering of the _reconquista_ led to a revival of the old crusading spirit, and the Order's Constable Alvaro de Luna (Master from 1445) won a great victory at Higuera in 1431. Significantly, he was executed after a palace revolution in 1453. From 1485 the mastership of the Order was reserved for the crown.

The castle and covered bridge to the sewage tower at Marienwerder (now Kwidzyn) in Poland, built by the Teutonic Knights from *c*.1233 onwards.

The Évora and Aviz Orders

As early as 1162 a small group of Portuguese knights known as the Brethren of Santa Maria was guarding the open plains of the Alemtejo province. In 1170 they obtained from King Alfonso an *encomienda* at Évora, 100 miles south-east of Lisbon, and adopted the Benedictine rule. The Order was too weak to maintain the *encomienda*, however, and Évora was handed over to the Templars, the Knights of Évora then coming under the jurisdiction of the Order of Calatrava.

After the Moorish invasion of Portugal in 1190 many *encomiendas* were built north of the Tagus, and in 1211 Alfonso II gave the Order the town of Aviz. The brethren then took the name the Knights of Aviz.

In 1218 the Order of Calatrava gave all its Portuguese property to the Knights of Aviz, and from then on, although still theoretically part of the Order of Calatrava, the Knights of Aviz became an independent order once more. The Order declined during the 15th century, and in 1496 its brethren were given permission to marry.

Details of the mantle worn by the Order are not known, but being under the Benedictine rule it would presumably have been black. Alfonso IV obtained papal permission for the Order to wear a green cross early in the 14th century.

The Knights of St Julian and Alcantara

In about 1166 a small group of knights known as the Knights of San Julian de Pereiro was operating on the frontier of Léon and Castile. In 1176 they were granted lands by Ferdinand II of Léon, and were recognised as a religious order by the Pope in 1183.

In 1187 the Order, needing the support of a more powerful body, placed itself under the jurisdiction of the Knights of Calatrava, although it retained its own elected Prior. In 1217 Alfonso of Léon gave

Alcantara to the Knights of Calatrava, but the following year this Order ceded the town and all its other possessions in Léon to the Order of St Julian, which was then renamed the Order of the Knights of Alcantara. By 1234 the Order could muster 600 knights and 2,000 foot soldiers.

Like the other Spanish orders, Alcantara was gradually taken over by the Crown, and its last Master died in 1494.

The *caballeros* and *clerigos* of the Order wore a plain black habit without insignia, but by about 1400 began to use a green cross fleury, in which the leaves of the fleur-de-lis curved back to touch the stem, as in the cross of the Knights of Calatrava.

The Knights of Our Lady of Montjoie

This Order was founded *circa* 1176 in the Holy Land by a Spaniard, Count Rodrigo, a former knight of Santiago. Rodrigo gave the Order lands in Castile and Aragon, and the king of Jerusalem gave the knights several towers to garrison in Ascalon. The Order's headquarters were at Montjoie, a castle on a hill outside Jerusalem. The Order was recognised by the Pope in 1180, and followed the Cistercian rule. It was intended to be an international order, but had difficulty in attracting recruits, and remained almost entirely Spanish. The knights wore a white habit with a red and white cross, the form of which is unknown.

A small detachment represented the Order at Hattin, and died there to a man. The survivors of the Order are supposed to have retired to Aragon, but at least a handful appear to have remained in the Holy Land, joining the Templars. In Aragon the Order became known as the Order of Trufac, but in 1221 Fernando of Aragon ordered it to be incorporated with the Knights of Calatrava.

The Mercedarians

This was an Aragonese order founded in 1233 by a Provençal nobleman., Père Nolasco, to ransom penniless Christian slaves. This rôle led to their also rescuing slaves and pilgrims by force where possible, and the Order soon became a military one, the clerics not regaining prominence until *circa* 1317 (see also Montesa).

The Order was never very numerous, and was able to field only small contingents of knights. They wore a white habit, and had a small shield bearing

Frontis of 1679 edition of *Chronicle of Prussia* by **Fra. Petrus von Düsburg** (*c.*1330), **shown in monastic habit on the right. On the left is the Hochmeister Fra. Werner von Orselen (1324-30) shown in armour of the late 17th century.**

the royal arms of Aragon on a neck chain.

The Knights of St George of Alfama

This Spanish order was founded in Aragon *circa* 1200, and followed the Augustinian rule. The Order does not seem to have thrived, or to have accomplished much, yet was not taken under the control of the Montesa Order (see below) until 1400. The brethren wore a white habit but do not seem to have used an insignia until the union with Montesa, when they adopted the cross of that Order.

The Knights of Christ

The dissolution of the Templars in 1312 led King Dinis of Portugal to create this order in 1318 to prevent the Order of St John from becoming too powerful in his kingdom. By 1321 the new order had 69 knights, nine chaplains, and six sergeants. Henri the Navigator became Master of the Order at the beginning of the 15th century; during his reign of office the Order employed the foremost geographers

Frontis of the rule of the Order of Santiago, illustrating the *espada* **insignia of the Order. (Courtesy the Capponi Collection)**

of the day, and its ships carried out expeditions which were half-missionary and half-commercial. By 1425 the Order had colonised Madeira and the Canaries; in 1445 it settled the Azores, and carried out a systematic exploration of the west coast of Africa. Vasco da Gama was a knight of the Order when in 1499 he sailed to India via the Cape of Good Hope.

However, by the first quarter of the 16th century the Order had so declined that the brethren were allowed to marry, and had also shed their vow of poverty.

The knights wore a white mantle or cloak with a 'red cross with a white twist in the middle', which has also been translated as 'a double cross of red and silver'.

The Knights of Our Lady of Montesa

This was an Aragonese order founded *circa* 1326 to take the place of the dissolved Templars. The Order took its name from its headquarters in Valencia, and at first was mainly formed from knights from the Order of Calatrava, and some Mercedarians whose Order had now ceased to be a military one. The white mantle of Calatrava was retained, but with a black cross. When the Order was merged with that of St George of Alfama *circa* 1400 it appears to have adopted a red cross as an insignia. The last Master died in 1589.

The Order of St James of Altopascio

This order, commonly known as the Order of the Tau from its insignia, is considered by some authors to be the oldest of all military orders, yet it has been ignored by English writers until now. Around the mid-10th century a hospital was founded at Altopascio near Lucca by some Augustinian monks with the intention of giving assistance to pilgrims making their way by this route to Rome or Santiago de Compostella. The first document mentioning this hospital dates back to the year 952. The next document is dated 1056, by which time the Order had *de facto* become military, for the monks had begun to provide an armed escort for the passage of pilgrims along the still uncivilised route between Lucca and Genoa. However, the main rôle of the Order remained non-military. The rule of the Order was not approved by the Pope until 1239, by which date the concept of military orders was well established.

Other hospitals were built in various parts of Europe, including France and England (a 'Hospital of Highgate'—a translation of Altopasso, later corrupted to Altopascio—still existed at Islington in 1626) but the Order was never very numerous or widely distributed. The waning of religious fervour and of pilgrimage led to its decline.

From 1446 to 1537 the mastership (Rector et Magister) was in the hands of the Capponi family of Florence, patrons of the Order. In 1537 the patronage and mastership passed to the Grifoni family after a dispute with Pope Paul III, who excommunicated the last Capponi Master for refusing to relinquish the office to one of the Pope's nephews. In 1585 the Order was absorbed by the Knights of St Stephen of Tuscany on the command of the Grand Duke Cosimo de'Medici.

The Knights of the Tau wore a habit of either very dark grey or black. The white truncated or 'tau' cross insignia of the Order was worn on the left breast. The hood of the habit was probably red, again with a white 'tau' cross.

The Knights of San Stefano of Tuscany

This Order was founded in 1561 by the Grand Duke Cosimo de'Medici of Tuscany to suppress corsairs. The Order followed the Benedictine rule, with the Grand Dukes as patrons and Masters. There were four classes of brethren: knights—who had to be of noble blood; chaplains; serving brethren; and cannonesses. The Order's headquarters, consisting of a church and convent, were built at Pisa.

The Order's galleys co-operated with those of the Knights of Malta in patrolling the Mediterranean, and 12 galleys of the Order fought at the decisive battle of Lepanto in 1571 when the Turks finally lost control of the Mediterranean.

The knights wore a white cloak lined in pale red, with a red, gold-edged Maltese cross on the left breast. The serving brethren wore a white cloak or tunic with a plain red cross; the chaplains, white with a red cross edged with yellow.

Effigy of Frey Martin Vasquez de Arce of the Order of Santiago, killed before Granada in 1486. From his tomb in the cathedral at Siguenza. Note the mantle with central *espada* **insignia of the Order, and the use of scale armour even at this late date.**

Sources

R. Barber, *The Knight and Chivalry* (London, 1970)

T. S. R. Boase, *Kingdoms and strongholds of the Crusaders* (London, 1971)

E. Bradford, *The Shield and the Sword: the Knights of Malta* (London, 1972)

Rev. E. L. Cutts, *Scenes and characters of the Middle Ages* (London, 1890)

Lt.Col. G. R. Gayre, *The Heraldry of the Knights of St John* (Allahabad, 1956)

H. W. Koch, *A History of Prussia* (London, 1978)

D. W. Lomax, *The Reconquista of Spain* (London, 1978)

J. Prawer, *The Latin Kingdom of Jerusalem* (London, 1972)

J. Prawer, *The World of the Crusaders* (London, 1972)

J. Riley-Smith, *The Knights of St John in Jerusalem and Cyprus, 1050–1310* (London, 1967)

R. Rudorff, *The Knights and their World* (London, 1974)

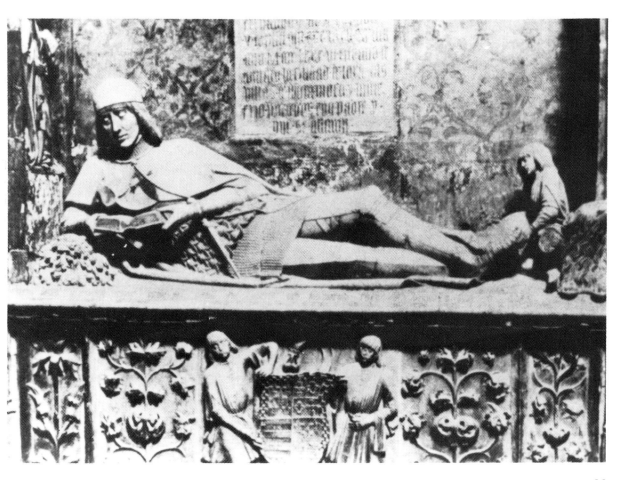

D. Seward, *The Monks of War* (London, 1972)

R. C. Smail, *Crusading Warfare 1097–1193* (Cambridge, 1956)

H. von. Treitschke (trans Paul), *Origins of Prussianism: the Teutonic Knights* (London, 1942)

T. Wise, *Wars of the Crusades, 1096–1291* (London, 1978)

The author also wishes to express his thanks to Niccolo Capponi of Florence, who so generously supplied information on the Order of St James of Altopascio.

The Plates

A1: Knight Hospitaller, 12th–13th centuries

This knight wears typical crusading gear: flat-topped 'great helm', kite shield with rounded top, all-mail armour, and long surcoat. Both the Benedictine and Augustinian habits were black, and as the Hospitallers followed the rule of these Orders their mantle was also black from the very beginning. Between 1120 and 1160 it was laid down that a white cross should be worn on the breast of this mantle to distinguish the Order. No example of this cross survives from the 12th century, but in 1224 the Master's seal showed a plain Latin cross as illustrated here. The cumbersome mantle was replaced in 1248 by a black surcoat with the white cross on the breast.

The banner illustrated is that attributed to the 'Knights of the Holy Sepulchre' (see text under Hospitallers).

A2: Turcopole, 12th–13th centuries

Turcopoles were Syrian mercenaries employed by the Military Orders during the crusades period to provide mounted archers. Contemporary sources describe them as 'light-armed', and this figure is based on these descriptions. The quilted aketon is the most likely form of body armour, aketon being a corruption of 'al-Qutun', the name of the quilted armour worn by many Saracens for its combination of lightness and strength. A small shield was also carried, which may have been painted to distinguish the Military Order to which the turcopole belonged. A light lance may have been used; the

turcopoles sometimes rode in the second rank of a cavalry formation to support the knights, although this was not their main rôle.

Effigy of Don Alvaro de Luna, Master of Santiago 1445–52, Constable of Castile and virtual ruler of that kingdom for almost 35 years. Note *espada* **insignia on breast.**

A3: Foot soldier, 12th–13th centuries

This figure is based on contemporary descriptions, with detail taken from the Maciejowski Bible, c.1250 (M638, f.27). Mercenary infantry had always been employed by the crusaders, and were either spearmen or crossbowmen. This figure wears typical equipment for both: quilted body armour over a long surcoat, kettle helmet, mail leggings, and a large shield bearing the identifying cross and colours of the Order.

B1: Knight Templar, c.1150

The Templars were granted permission by the Pope in 1145 to wear a white, hooded mantle similar to that of the Cistercians. This was replaced on active service by a white cloak, probably worn over a surcoat. From the time of the Second Crusade (1147) a red cross was worn on the left breast and on the shield; sergeants wore a brown mantle or cloak with the same cross on the left breast. The banner of the Templars was known as the Beauséant. The lance pennons of the knights were white, charged with the cross of the Order.

B2: Pilgrim

Contemporary accounts refer to pilgrims as wearing a grey-coloured, shaggy wool robe and a round felt hat with a brim; also as being barefoot, although sandals would have seemed an essential for the long distances covered on foot. Pilgrims usually vowed not to cut their hair or beard until their pilgrimage was accomplished. Other marks of the pilgrim were a staff, some five to seven feet long, with a hook for a water bottle or bundle, and a scrip or small bag for food and other necessities. The scrip shown here bears the scallop-shell badge of a pilgrim who has been to the shrine of St James at Compostella. The scallop-shell is a common charge in the arms of English knights, many of whom stopped off en route to the Holy Land to serve against the Moors in Spain under the banner of the Order of Santiago.

B3: Knight Templar, late 13th century

John of Dreux, who lived in 1275, is here dressed in the manner normal for knights within their preceptories. The detail is drawn from the effigy on his tombstone. Confrère knights were not allowed to wear the white mantle. Beards were compulsory in

Calatrava la Nueva, headquarters of the Knights of Calatrava from c.1216 onwards.

all three of the main military orders in the Holy Land—Hospitallers, Templars and Teutonic—and indeed, the warrior-monks took pride in a dishevelled appearance.

C1: Teutonic Knight, c.1230

The Teutonic Knights appear to have worn a white cloak or surcoat with a black Latin cross from about 1191. The cross was repeated on the knight's shield. This figure's clothing and armour are typical of the crusading period. Note the presence of a heavily padded arming cap under the mail coif.

C2: Teutonic Knight, c.1300

This figure is a confrère knight—the famous minnesinger Tannhauser—from the equally famous Manessa Codex. Confrère knights were allowed to bear their own arms on their shields. The original painting shows the cross of the Order on the right breast of the mantle, contrary to other sources. The headgear is difficult to interpret, even from the original. It is definitely of 'pill-box' design, but the white drapery around it may be a pillow and have nothing to do with the hat itself. If that were so, then the 'pill-box' would resemble closely the caps shown on warrior monks in other sources: e.g. see B3.

C3: Sergeant, Teutonic Order, c.1230

Sergeants of the Order wore a grey surcoat or cloak, bearing a truncated form of cross. This figure bears the simple banner of the Order and wears the normal armour for the period. Note that the shield is the transitional, truncated form of kite shield, which evolved into the heater shield, shown with C2. A surviving heater shield measures 95 cms in length, though this may not have been the norm.

D1: Knight of Santiago, 13th century

Knights of Santiago wore a white habit with a red cross on the left breast. The bottom arm of the cross

Romantic portrayals of knights of military orders, from a 19th century Spanish work on military history; although the costumes are fanciful, the insignia beneath the figures are a useful reference. The Orders of Salvador and Encina have not been identified.

resembled a sword blade, and this form of cross became known as the cross *espada*. At some point in the first quarter of the 15th century a black tunic was adopted, with the red espada on the chest. The Portuguese Order of Sao Thiago also wore a white habit, but the bottom arm of their cross ended in a fleur-de-lis. Note the distinctive shield and simple iron cap of the Spanish knight, based on details in a contemporary manuscript commissioned by King James of Aragon.

D2: Frey Martin Vasquez de Arce

This figure is a *frey-caballero* of the Order of Santiago, who was killed before Granada in 1486. This reconstruction is based on his tomb effigy in the cathedral at Siguenza. Note the use of scale body armour at this late date. Light armour remained quite common in warmer climates such as Spain and Italy, and it is likely that lighter equipments were worn by many of the knights on Rhodes and Malta.

D3: Frey Don Alvaro de Luna

This figure is Master of the Order of Santiago,

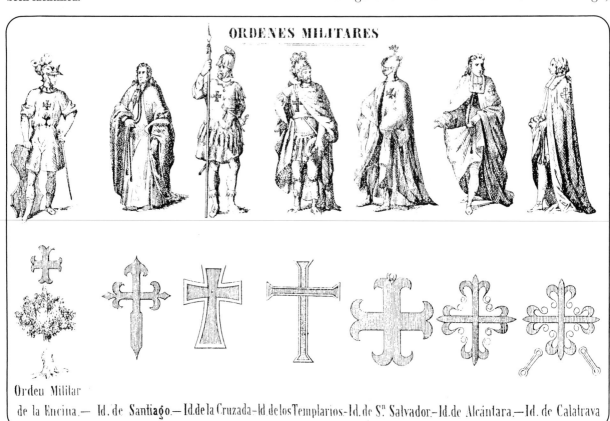

ORDENES MILITARES

Orden Militar de la Encina.— Id. de Santiago.— Id.de la Cruzada.—Id. de los Templarios.—Id. de Sn. Salvador.—Id.de Alcántara.—Id. de Calatrava

36

1445–53, based on the *retablo* by Sancho de Zamora in the chapel of Santiago, at Toledo cathedral. He wears the gilded full plate armour of the Master, with the white mantle and red espada of the Order. No illustration exists of the Order's banner, but at the fall of Seville in 1248 it was described thus: 'The Master planted the red damask standard of St James and the white horse high on the city walls.'

E1: Knight Hospitaller, early 14th century

This figure is taken from a contemporary manuscript in the British Museum (Royal 1696, f.335), showing the Prior of the Hospital at Jerusalem and the Master of the Templars before the king of France. Beside the Prior is the figure illustrated here, identified as Raymond du Puy. In 1259, as a result of a petition by the Hospitallers, permission was granted for all military brethren to wear surcoats 'and other military insignia which shall be of a red colour, and in which a white coloured cross is placed, in the same manner as in your standard.' The Pope also confirmed an attempt to differentiate knights and sergeants by not granting the red surcoat to the latter; but in the statute of 1278 it was laid down that *all* brethren at arms were to wear the red surcoat, and all brethren to wear the black mantle. The Order's cross had now taken the shape of a cross formée.

The Order's banner, one form of which is illustrated here, was granted in 1130 and remained

Commandery of the Order of Santiago at Segura de la Sierra, Jaén.

Seals of the Order of Altopascio, illustrating various forms of 'tau' cross, the insignia of the Order.

unchanged throughout the Order's history. The swallow-tailed lance pennons of the knights were emblazoned with the same cross and colours. There was a guidon version for the Order's ships when it became a naval power.

E2: Knight Hospitaller, c.1530
The figure has been dated by its clubbed shoes. The habit remained monastic, but the knights now followed more closely the current fashions in clothing, and dressed much more richly than in previous centuries. A feather was frequently worn with such hats.

E3: Knight Hospitaller, mid-16th century
Knights of the Military Orders also followed the fashion in arms and armour, and this knight illustrates how the advent of effective gunpowder weapons had led to the abandoning of much armour. The 'braided' armour, open-faced burgeonet, and unarmoured legs are typical of the equipment worn by knights during the sieges of Rhodes and Malta. This particular figure is based on an illustration on the title page of a contemporary book.

F1: Hochmeister of the Teutonic Order, mid-15th century
This figure is clad in the type of armour worn during the first half of the 15th century for fighting on foot. The visored and articulated sallet and the poleaxe both date from c.1455. The tunic of the Hochmeister is based on a contemporary description, and bears the Imperial eagle granted to the Order by the Holy Roman Emperor in 1226.

F2: Fra Petrus von Düsburg, c.1330
This figure is portrayed as he appears in the frontispiece to the 1679 edition of his *Chronicle of Prussia*. The banner is based on a contemporary description following its capture at the battle of Tannenberg in 1410.

F3: Fra Kuno von Liebensteyn, died 1391
This figure is taken from his brass at Nowemiasto in Poland, which was made at the Marienburg. He wears burnished plate armour, bascinet and aventail, and the white tunic of the Teutonic Order. The pavise is also in the Order's colours.

G1, 2, 3: Master and two knights of the Order of St John
These figures are depicted at the siege of Rhodes in 1480, and are taken from a late 15th century manuscript. All three wear a mixture of plate armour and civilian dress, but the insignia of their Order remains the dominant factor. The tabard-style garment worn over their armour was either studded or decorated in gold, and frequently bore religious 'slogans'.

H1: Sir Thomas Docwra
This knight was the Grand Prior of the Order of St John in England, 1501–1527, and his likeness is taken from a contemporary engraving. The Order reached the height of its prosperity in England under Sir Thomas, a renowned soldier and diplomat who stood high in the favour of Henry VII and Henry VIII.

H2: Philip de l'Isle Adam
The famous Grand Master of the Order of St John, 1521–34, as portrayed in a painting of his arrival in Malta. Note the clubbed shoes and white ruff of the period; and the richness of the mantle, which is now civilian in style, no longer monastic.

H3: Knight of Malta (St John), 17th century
This knight is taken from an anonymous portrait in the Stibbert Museum, Florence. Note the large cross of the Order on the breastplate: this was the size preferred by the Order. The remainder of the knight's clothing is typical for any soldier of the first half of the 17th century.

INDEX

Figures in **bold** refer to illustrations